SEP 2 9 2003

P9-BYW-008

Explore Space!

Neil Armstrong

by Thomas Streissguth

Consultant:
James Gerard
Aerospace Education Specialist
NASA Aerospace Education Services Program

Bridgestone Books
an imprint of Capstone Press
Mankato, Minnesota

Bridgestone Books are published by Capstone Press
151 Good Counsel Drive, P.O. Box 669, Mankato, Minnesota 56002
http://www.capstone-press.com

Library of Congress Cataloging-in-Publication Data
Streissguth, Thomas, 1958–
    Neil Armstrong / by Thomas Streissguth.
        p. cm.—(Explore space!)
    Summary: Presents a brief biography of the first astronaut to walk on the Moon.
    Includes bibliographical references and index.
    ISBN 0-7368-1627-5 (hardcover)
    1. Armstrong, Neil, 1930– —Juvenile literature. 2. Astronauts—United States—
Biography—Juvenile literature. [1. Armstrong, Neil, 1930– 2. Astronauts.] I. Title. II. Series.
TL789.85.A75 S74 2003
629.45′0092—dc21   2002010133

Editorial Credits

Chris Harbo and Roberta Schmidt, editors; Karen Risch, product planning editor; Steve
    Christensen, series designer; Juliette Peters, cover and interior designer; Alta Schaffer,
    photo researcher

Photo Credits

Corbis/Bettmann, 8
NASA, cover, 4, 10, 12, 14, 16, 18, 20
Neil Armstrong Air and Space Museum/Paul Nagel, 6 (both)
PhotoDisc, 6 (background)

1 2 3 4 5 6 08 07 06 05 04 03

Table of Contents

Neil Armstrong

Neil Armstrong loves to fly. In the 1950s, he worked as a U.S. Navy test pilot. Neil's most famous mission was the space flight of *Apollo 11* in 1969. Neil became the first person to walk on the Moon.

test pilot
a pilot who tests new airplanes

Learning to Fly

Neil Alden Armstrong was born August 5, 1930. He grew up in Wapakoneta, Ohio. He loved airplanes. At age 15, Neil took flying lessons. Neil earned a pilot's license before he earned his driver's license.

license
a document that allows a person to do something

During the Korean War, Neil flew F9F *Panthers* like the ones pictured here. These airplanes took off from and landed on boats called carriers.

Wartime Service

In 1949, Neil joined the U.S. Navy. He served as a fighter pilot during the Korean War (1950–1953). He flew 78 missions. Neil earned three medals for his skill and courage in Korea. After the war, Neil attended Purdue University. In 1955, he earned an engineering degree.

engineering
the science of designing and building machines or structures

Test Pilot

After college, Neil worked as a test pilot. He flew high-speed planes. One of these planes was the X-15. This rocket-powered plane could fly almost 4,000 miles (6,400 kilometers) an hour. Neil flew the X-15 seven times.

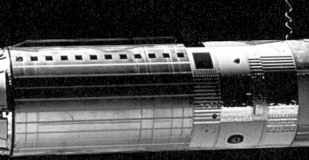
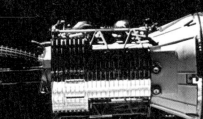

NASA launched 12 Gemini missions between 1964 and 1966. These missions helped scientists learn about space travel.

NASA Astronaut

In 1962, Neil became an astronaut for NASA's Gemini program. Neil's first mission was in 1966. He docked *Gemini 8* with a satellite. But the spacecraft began to spin out of control. Neil solved the problem and brought *Gemini 8* safely back to Earth.

dock
when one spacecraft connects with another spacecraft

Millions of people watched Neil's first steps on the Moon on TV. As he climbed down the ladder, Neil said, "That's one small step for man, one giant leap for mankind."

Apollo 11

On July 16, 1969, NASA launched *Apollo 11*. Neil, Michael Collins, and Buzz Aldrin flew *Apollo 11* to the Moon. On July 20, Neil and Aldrin landed a lunar module on the Moon's surface. Neil and Aldrin explored the Moon's surface. They put up an American flag.

lunar module
a spacecraft that lands on the Moon

The Apollo Team

The *Apollo 11* mission was a team effort.
Neil was the mission commander.
Collins flew the *Apollo 11* spacecraft.
Aldrin flew the lunar module. Many
scientists at Misson Control also helped
the astronauts. During the landing, they
talked with Neil and Aldrin by radio.

Mission Control
a center at NASA where
people help astronauts
during missions

17

AEROSPACE WALK OF HONOR

IMAGINATION
REASON
SKILL

Neil Alden Armstrong

Neil Armstrong is best known as commander of the three-man team who, in 1969, piloted the first lunar landing module to the Moon's surface. "One small step for man, one giant leap for mankind," was the phrase Armstrong used to describe the historic Gemini 8 mission.

Armstrong logged over 6,000 hours of flight time in over 200 types of aircraft, including X-1B, F-100A, X-5, X-15, LLTV, F-101, F-102, F-5D-1, B-47, B-29, P-51 and the Paraglider.

He participated in more than 100 launches of rocket airplane flights. As the NASA project pilot on the X-15, he flew to 207,500 feet and 3,989

times and was selected as pilot for the Dynasoar experimental aircraft. After seven years as a test pilot he volunteered for the astronaut program (1962-1970).

He was backup command pilot for Gemini 5, Gemini 11 and Apollo 8. He was command pilot of Gemini 8 and the Apollo XI Lunar Mission. He was later named Deputy Associate Administrator for the NASA Aeronautics Office of Advanced Research and Technology.

Armstrong was born in Ohio in 1930. He received his BA from Purdue (1955) and MS from the University of Southern California (1970, both in Aeronautical Engineering. He served as professor of Aerospace Engineering at the University of Cin-

cinnati.

Armstrong is the recipient of three Air Medals and the Gold Space Medal. His other honors include Chanute Award, Kincheloe Award, Collier Trophy, Presidential Medal of Freedom, and the Aerospace Walk of Honor.

Established in 1990 by the Lancaster City Council, the Aerospace Walk of Honor celebrates test pilots who were associated with Edwards AFB. Recognition is awarded for distinguished aviation careers marked by significant and obvious achievements beyond one specific accomplishment.

AEROSPACE
WALK OF HONOR

Life After *Apollo 11*

Neil retired from NASA in 1971. He became an engineering teacher at the University of Cincinnati. Later, Neil worked for computer and engineering companies. Over the years, Neil received many honors for his space flights. Today, he lives on a farm near Lebanon, Ohio.

One Giant Leap

Apollo 11 was a success for Neil and for NASA. The mission proved that astronauts could explore the Moon and outer space. By 1972, NASA had sent five more missions to the Moon. The success of these missions excited people about outer space.

Important Dates

1930—Neil Alden Armstrong is born August 5.

1949—Neil becomes a U.S. Navy pilot. He flies 78 combat missions during the Korean War.

1955—Neil graduates from Purdue University. He then works as an engineer and test pilot at the Lewis Research Center in Cleveland, Ohio.

1962—Neil joins NASA as an astronaut in the Gemini space program.

1966—Neil flies aboard *Gemini 8*.

1969—Neil flies aboard *Apollo 11*. On July 20, he becomes the first person to walk on the Moon.

1971—Neil retires from NASA. He becomes an engineering teacher at the University of Cincinnati.

Present—Neil lives on a farm in Lebanon, Ohio.

Words to Know

astronaut (ASS-truh-nawt)—someone trained to fly into space in a spacecraft

commander (kuh-MAND-er)—an astronaut who is in charge of a space mission

courage (KUR-ij)—bravery in times of danger

degree (di-GREE)—a title given to a person for finishing a course of study in college

mission (MISH-uhn)—a planned job or task

retire (ri-TIRE)—to give up a line of work

satellite (SAT-uh-lite)—a machine that circles Earth; many satellites take pictures or send telephone calls and TV programs to Earth.

surface (SUR-fiss)—the top layer of something

Read More

Bredeson, Carmen. *Neil Armstrong: A Space Biography.*
Countdown to Space. Springfield, NJ: Enslow, 1998.
Brown, Don. *One Giant Leap: The Story of Neil Armstrong.*
Boston: Houghton Mifflin, 1998.

Internet Sites

Track down many sites about Neil Armstrong.
Visit the FACT HOUND at
http://www.facthound.com

IT IS EASY! IT IS FUN!

1) Go to *http://www.facthound.com*
2) Type in: 0736816275
3) Click on "FETCH IT" and FACT HOUND will find several
links hand-picked by our editors.

Relax and let our pal FACT HOUND do the research for you!

Index